The Leader-Post Carrier Foundation Inc. was established by Regina's daily newspaper as a tribute to its past and present carriers. The foundation is named in honour of the Leader-Post Carriers with the aim of supporting educational and humanitarian needs in southern Saskatchewan.

Individual and corporate donations help fund the Foundation, but its primary income is from the proceeds of special projects organized on behalf of the Foundation by *The Leader-Post.*

Among the most successful projects have been previous books: *Children's Medical Emergency Handbook; Cornerstones 1 and 2, An Artist's History of The City of Regina; Getting It Together; HomeTips: Organizing Strategies for a Streamlined Home Life; Household Hints – Environmental and Energy; Household Hints – Money and Time-Saving; WorkTips: Organizing Strategies for a Productive Work Life* and *A Year of Crafts.*

Prairie Pilgrimage is the Foundation's tenth publication. This book profiles prairie farm dwellings and former landmarks that have been abandoned as times change. Its proceeds will make a difference to the people who benefit from the Foundation's support.

Jack Pickering

A Prairie Romanticist

Jack Pickering's millennium project, which has culminated in *Prairie Pilgrimage – 366 Prairie Sketches*, is a natural progression of his lifetime of work as a prairie artist. From January 1 to December 31, 2000, each day he sketched a moment in time on the prairies, focusing on the evidence of human habitation.

Born and raised at Wilcox, Saskatchewan, Pickering has a family heritage of artistic accomplishment. His great-grandfather, Joseph L. Pickering, R.A., was widely recognized as an English Romanticist, a landscape artist who was most impressed with "the more rugged type of picturesqueness in which there is a note of natural tragedy." It was also said of him, "One of the greatest merits of his art is its entire absence of affectation."

Jack Pickering may now have earned an adaptation of his great-grandfather's title with this collection of sketches of abandoned and decaying prairie farmhouses, barns, churches and grain elevators. As a Prairie Romanticist he has interpreted the remains of buildings that remind us of the many once-flourishing farms and small communities that dotted the vast prairies. Over the last century they have succumbed to drought, population shifts and a changing economy. Once abandoned, the forces of a relentless prairie climate turned them into crumbling silent sentinals of prairie history.

PRAIRIE
PILGRIMAGE
366 PRAIRIE SKETCHES

Best Wishes
J L Pickering

BY JACK L. PICKERING

The Tenth In The Best-Selling Series From The Publishers Of:
Children's Medical Emergency Handbook
Cornerstones 1 – An Artist's History of the City of Regina
Cornerstones 2 – An Artist's History of the City of Regina
Getting It Together
Home Tips – How to Organize Your Home and Personal Life
Household Hints – Environmental and Energy
Household Hints – Money and Time-Saving
Work Tips – How to Organize Your Professional and Business Life
A Year of Crafts

Printed using vegetable-based (Canola) inks

Prairie Pilgrimage – 366 Prairie Sketches

by Jack L. Pickering

First Printing – October 2001

Canadian Cataloguing in Publication Data

Pickering, Jack L., 1928 –

Prairie pilgrimage – 366 prairie sketches

ISBN 1-894022-71-8

1. Saskatchewan – Pictorial works. 2. Farm buildings – Saskatchewan – Pictorial works. I. Title.
FC3512.P52 2001 971.24'009173'4 C2001-911569-5
F1071.8.P52 2001

Formatting and page design by Iona Glabus

Printed and Produced in Canada by
Centax Books, A Division of PWGroup
Publishing Director – Margo Embury
1150 Eighth Avenue, Regina, Saskatchewan
Canada S4R 1C9
(306) 525-2304 Fax (306) 757-2439
E-mail: centax@printwest.com www.centaxbooks.com

Thousands of people have unknowingly admired many of Pickering's earlier paintings. For 22 years he created background paintings and displays at the Royal Saskatchewan Museum. He also illustrated museum publications and created numerous interpretive dioramas and displays for provincial parks in Saskatchewan. His current project is with the Duck Lake Museum, a design for their tower. Even though he is officially retired, he recently designed and painted the background for the Fraser Lake exhibit at the Royal Saskatchewan Museum.

Pickering has had one-man and group exhibitions of his watercolours, oils, acrylics, pencil sketches and bronze sculptures in Alberta, British Columbia, Ontario and Saskatchewan. His work has been exhibited with the Canada Nature Art exhibit and featured at fundraisers for Ducks Unlimited. Copies of one of his bronze sculptures, of a sharp-tailed grouse – Saskatchewan's provincial bird, were presented to each of the provincial premiers when they attended a premier's conference in Saskatoon. Although he is largely self-taught, Pickering has also been an art instructor. He does accept commissions for sketches of individual houses, barns and farmyards.

Jack Pickering was born on his parents' first farm near Avonlea (Sec. 24, Tp. 12, Rge 22, W.2 Sask.) and grew up on their farm near Wilcox. Ironically, it and the outlying buildings, granaries and a barn, have been vacant since the 1960s, peopled only with memories. Pickering can relate personally to the deserted buildings he has immortalized in his sketches and the lives that were once lived within them. In *Prairie Pilgrimage – 366 Prairie Sketches* his keen eye and his artistry provide a record of what once was and will soon be gone – prairie history in transition.

Introduction

The year 2000 has been very rewarding. My personal millennium project, which has resulted in this book, *Prairie Pilgrimage – 366 Prairie Sketches*, was to complete a sketch a day for the entire year. 2000 was a leap year, thus 366 sketches.

On New Year's Day the first sketch was of our birdfeeder in the backyard. From that time on I drove out into the countryside, selecting subjects that interested me.

Later, in the month of March, I noticed that many buildings or landmarks had disappeared and others were in imminent danger of disappearing. I decided to devote the rest of the project to buildings such as houses, barns, granaries, grain elevators and a few churches. Each had its own character; in addition to the original architecture, time and the prairie climate had effected many changes. Some buildings were leaning, sagging, minus shingles, glass, paint, and in various stages of deterioration.

Over the course of the year I drove many miles, at times returning to the same area to travel another low road in search of another building. My binoculars were a great aid in scanning the countryside.

The winter of 2000 was ideal, very little snow and most of the time above normal temperatures. Summer was another matter, as we had abundant rain, twenty some inches in some areas. Under these conditions I had to choose mainly grid or blacktop roads to locate new subject matter.

In the first six months, I would pack a lunch and head out with a package of precut drawing paper, pencils, paper stomps (for shading), and several types of erasers. For the last six months, I used my camera and worked from the photos.

In most of the sketches I've added very simple skies of the day to give an overall atmospheric feeling. My idea of a sketch is not to include every detail in the drawing, but to eliminate and simplify, keeping in mind the main focal point. A simple sketch of just a few lines can create an impression. If the impression makes the viewer think and remember, or wonder about the lives lived within some of these abandoned houses or the history of the rural churches and other buildings, then it has all been worthwhile.

As I sketched many old houses, in unfamiliar areas, I wondered who had lived there in the early years and thought of the hardships those people endured; the long cold, snowy winters; the dry years; the infestations of grasshoppers and army worms. I also thought of the many happy times that these buildings had witnessed: the family holiday dinners; the weddings; the births.

As each old farmstead disappears, in what some call progress, with the continuing evolution toward larger farms, etc., the history of these vacant buildings is lost forever.

The one-room schools, with one teacher instructing up to eight grades, were the first to disappear. Many children have no idea where their grandparents lived or the name or location of the schools they attended.

The country elevators are being destroyed, eliminating many town and village landmarks. In most prairie towns the elevators, with the highly visible town names printed on each one, were the dominant features. When you travel in the country today, if you miss the small town sign on the highway (if there are any) you have no idea what town or village you have passed through.

Many communities are no longer on our Saskatchewan road maps. In a drive from Weyburn to Moose Jaw via highway #39 I can name four – Ibsen, Diana, Pitman and Stelcam. Pitman at one time had an elevator, general store, post office and a farm fuel agent.

I hope some readers can recognize their family homes or other buildings in these sketches and reflect back to times gone by.

Completing my objective required dedication, discipline and determination to see this project through to year's end. I had many pleasureable experiences exploring the prairie byways, discovering forgotten buildings and preserving their memory by committing their images to paper. Family visits to Springside, Melfort, Katepwa campground and Calgary also provided resources along the way for some of the sketches.

May I at this time thank my wife, Clarese, and extend my appreciation to her and my family for their encouragement, patience and understanding while I completed my Prairie Pilgrimage.

H. Pickering

The beginning of my sketch-a-day-for-the-year-2000 project. I've been feeding birds in the winter for over 20 years. Over this time we've had various species such as sparrows, house finches, red polls, pine siskins, etc. A red-breasted nuthatch and a blue jay both spent one entire winter enjoying our feeding station. *(Jan. 1, 2000)*

Silhouetted against a sunset sky, this threshing machine stands in a fence corner on a hilltop in Springside, Saskatchewan. *(Jan. 2, 2000)*

These outbuildings are all that is left of a farmyard southwest of Milestone. *(Jan. 3, 2000)*

A coyote hunts for a meal in a slough southwest of Milestone. He blends into the background of dock. *(Jan. 4, 2000)*

The RY Trail – early in the
twentieth century this was the road from Regina to
Yellowstone in the U.S., and it is still referred to as such. The landscape
drops into a treed coulee, a yearly home for black-billed magpies.
(Jan. 5, 2000)

I sketched these buildings with distant hills on a cold,
crisp January morning southwest of Milestone.
(Jan. 6, 2000)

On my drive this morning along the RY Trail,
I came upon this sharp-tailed grouse sitting on a gate fence post.
Although hunting season was over the bird emphasized the fact that he was in safe territory. *(Jan. 7, 2000)*

It is unusual not to see a snowy owl on a winter's drive. This female sits atop a round plywood grain bin west of Milestone, watching for mice or voles in the snow. *(Jan. 8, 2000)*

Bethesda Lutheran church southwest of Wilcox is a directional landmark in the community. I attended church and Sunday school here as a boy. *(Jan. 9, 2000)*

All that stands in this farmyard west of Milestone is the house and the dilapidated old garage. The barn collapsed long ago. *(Jan. 10, 2000)*

Edwin Anderson's metal-clad
house still stands southwest of Wilcox.
(Jan. 11, 2000)

The house and barn are all that remain of the Pickering farm
southwest of Wilcox. My parents moved there in 1937.
It has been vacant since the 1960s.
(Jan. 12, 2000)

This poplar tree growing in a ditch west of Milestone grew from seed blown by the wind or dropped by a bird. A short-eared owl scans the area for lunch. *(Jan. 13, 2000)*

In the same location as the previous sketch, this landscape shows poplar trees growing as nature planted them. A fox hunts among the dock.
(Jan. 14, 2000)

Red willows and hawthorn line the banks of the Moose Jaw River west of Milestone. A great area for white-tailed deer, they yard up here for winter. *(Jan. 15, 2000)*

A stormy winter day, with high winds and drifting snow, south of Wilcox. No matter which direction I looked, the blowing snow wiped out almost everything in the landscape. *(Jan. 16, 2000)*

This cement bridge spans the Moose Jaw River west of Milestone. Visibility is very poor again today. *(Jan. 17, 2000)*

This sketch depicts poplar groves in the Caledonia Elmsthorpe community pasture, named for those municipalities. This area is noted for its birds, upland plovers, horned owls, tree swallows, yellow-shafted flickers, magpies, Swainson's hawks, and various grasslands birds, just to name a few. *(Jan. 18, 2000)*

An old oxbow in the Moose Jaw River west of Milestone, in June you might observe a white-tailed deer and her fawn in this area. *(Jan. 19, 2000)*

A total lunar eclipse of the moon as seen from our upper deck – this is the only sketch in which I included some colour. This sketch is special as it was done on our daughter Connie's birthday. *(Jan. 20, 2000)*

This old horse-drawn disc, southwest of Milestone, is evidence of another era. Note the rocks and weights to assist penetration of the disc into the hard soil. *(Jan. 21, 2001)*

Near the location of the previous sketch, I was fascinated with snow shadows on a bright winter afternoon. *(Jan. 22, 2000)*

These old corrals are in a small pasture southwest of Milestone. *(Jan. 23, 2000)*

This part of the Moose Jaw River south of Wilcox is lined with cattails. *(Jan. 24, 2000)*

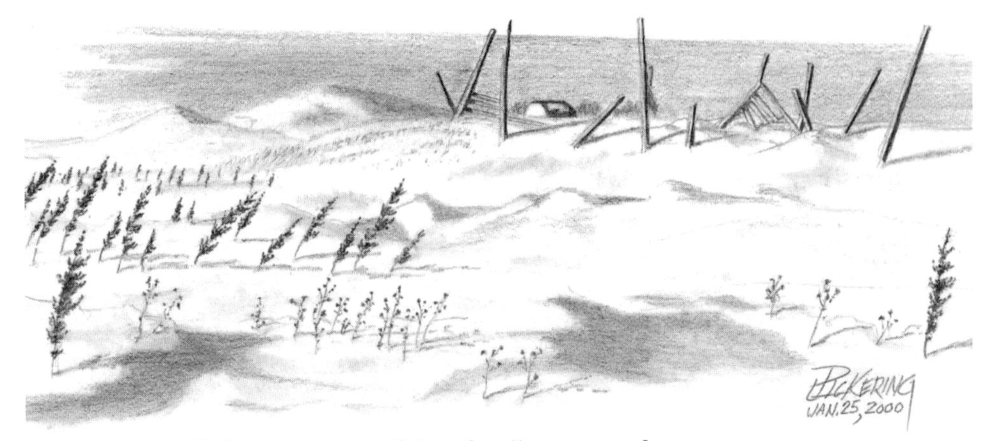

All that remains of this feedlot west of Milestone are a few poles and boards. They created an interesting composition with Don Anderson's barn framed in the distance between the poles. *(Jan. 25, 2000)*

This weathered white barn southwest of Lang was constructed by a Mr. Monson. *(Jan. 26, 2000)*

A great horned owl nested for several years near this faded blue shed located south of Milestone.

(Jan. 27, 2000)

Deep shadows create a strong contrast on a sunny January afternoon southeast of Milestone.

(Jan. 28, 2000)

This dilapidated barn in much need of repair is located in a little hollow east of Bengough. *(Jan. 29, 2000)*

Another barn built by Mr. Monson, this one is located on his grandson Jim's farm southwest of Lang. *(Jan. 30, 2000)*

The Moorhead farm is located on a rise south of Milestone. The bright sun cast contrasting shadows on the cream-coloured stucco house. *(Jan. 31, 2000)*

Another lone poplar tree, the town of Wilcox is on the horizon. *(Feb. 1, 2000)*

All that remains of my Grandfather's homestead west of Milestone is the treed yard to the right of the road leading west. The Smith farm is on the left, silhouetted against the Avonlea Blue Hills. *(Feb. 2, 2000)*

A close-up view of E.W. Smith's farmhouse west of my grandfather's homestead. *(Feb. 3, 2000)*

This beaver house, in the ditch east and south of Milestone, is on the edge of the Moose Jaw River. *(Feb. 4, 2000)*

These empty wooden grain bins southeast of Milestone are an interesting contrast to the three large steel bins in the centre of this sketch. *(Feb. 5, 2000)*

This old shop is located just north of the February 5 sketch. A pasture to the north with a winding creek is an ideal habitat for mule deer. *(Feb. 6, 2000)*

An old barn south of Milestone, sketched about 5 p.m., presents a stark silhouette at sunset. *(Feb. 7, 2000)*

Long shadows on a February afternoon on the Charlton farm south of Milestone.
(Feb. 8, 2000)

An old abandoned wagon left near the Moose Jaw River south of Milestone is inundated in the spring runoff, after heavy rains.
(Feb. 9, 2000)

Heavy blowing snow almost obliterates these small buildings located west of Milestone near a marsh surrounded by ever-present dockweeds. *(Feb. 10, 2000)*

The Stenseth farm west of Milestone in heavy blowing snow – years ago, as a boy, every Sunday afternoon during the summer I played softball with neighbours in a pasture just north of this yard. *(Feb. 11, 2000)*

I sketched my Grandfather's homestead house from an old photo taken about 1910 or 1911. The February 2 sketch shows the yard with trees. The new house shows the bottom area covered with tarpaper to keep out some of the floor drafts in winter. The house was located on the SE quarter Section 16, Township 12, Range 21, west of the second meridian.
(Feb. 12, 2000)

This harrow wheel drawbar was abandoned in a small creek. The Merv Phillips' farm to the northwest is located west of my grandfather's farm.
(Feb. 13, 2000)

This farmyard is located on the Avonlea highway #334. A pasture just north of these buildings was the last area where the locals played Sunday softball, after vacating the diamond at the Stenseth farm. *(Feb. 14, 2000)*

A male snowy owl is perched on a power pole, viewing a stubble field west of Milestone.
(Feb. 15, 2000)

On a trip
to Bengough, on
a cross-country road to
Hardy, I sketched this old house. Note the
ragged dark strips and dark patches. At one time the
exterior was covered with red rolled roofing. *(Feb. 16, 2000)*

Another early house located on the same road as the sketch of the 16th, the chimney appeared to be made of stone.
(Feb. 17, 2000)

The
former
farm of Ken
and Janice Braaten,
southwest of Milestone,
the only building that
remains is the white, red-
trimmed house. The red-painted wood
cutout butterflies reminded me of warmer
days to come. *(Feb. 18, 2000)*

A sketch of
the Bradley farm, the
nearest barn with its wooden roof
has collapsed, while the metal-clad roof to
the east of it is intact. This farm southwest of Milestone
can be dated to the early days of horsepower. *(Feb.19, 2000)*

The Tingvold farm is
southwest of Milestone. *(Feb. 20, 2000)*

The Cryer house is also southwest of Milestone.
(Feb. 21, 2000)

This house southwest of Milestone, with its brick asphalt siding, was the home of Ted Omoth. *(Feb. 22, 2000)*

This is all that remains of the
Oliver Omoth farm southwest of Milestone.
The barn is gone. Years ago my parents hauled
drinking water in a wooden barrel from the well near the barn. *(Feb. 23, 2000)*

As I made this sketch a heavy fog rolled in. The white house with green trim is southwest of Wilcox. Now vacant, it belonged to the Nygren family. *(Feb. 24, 2000)*

An evening sketch of a cattle shade located southwest of Milestone, note the short-eared owl. They are nocturnal and hunt at night. *(Feb. 25, 2000)*

I couldn't resist doing a sketch of four mule deer feeding in the morning west of Milestone. The Lutheran Church and the Hval farm are on the distant horizon. *(Feb. 26, 2000)*

This weathered red barn is located on highway #6 south of Milestone. *(Feb. 27, 2000)*

The Moreland Federal elevator on highway #6 in the Parry area has been closed for years. A designated historic sign lists Redrose, Wildrose, Fordyce and Kenneth as School Districts of the area before consolidation and larger units were introduced.
(Feb. 28, 2000)

This farmyard with the faded white barn and sway-backed grain bin west of Milestone was owned by George Nelson.
(Feb. 29, 2000)

This weather worn barn, originally owned by the Satherlies, stands a mile and a half from the Pickering farm. Jenny Satherlie was my Grades 1 and 2 teacher at Vimy School. *(Mar.1, 2000)*

While sitting in my car northeast of Long Creek Golf Course, just off highway #334, doing this sketch of the Ennich farm, Norm Thompson, a R.C.M.P. officer from Avonlea, pulled up thinking I was having problems. In our discussion he informed me he was a relative of Tom Thompson the famous Group of Seven artist. *(Mar. 2, 2000)*

Located just off the Dummer Grid west of highway #6, this barn and collapsed chicken house are all that remain on this property.

(Mar. 3, 2000)

Traveling
west of the March 3 sketch, this small
cottage-roofed house, the early home of Norman
Kesslering, stands in a spruce treed yard. *(Mar. 4, 2000)*

On a road north of Dummer, on the banks of the Avonlea Creek, is the original home of the Paulsrud family.
(Mar. 5. 2000)

This set of buildings south of Milestone, belonging to Edna Bradley, sits above the bank of the Moose Jaw River. Note steps leading down to the river. Bright afternoon sunlight casts a shadow on the house from the large poplar tree to the left.
(Mar. 6, 2000)

PICKERING
MAR.6,2000

This green-trimmed white house, and garage,
located southwest of Milestone is where the Dicken family lived.
(Mar. 7, 2000)

This barn with a high sliding door was converted
into a machine shed. On a road north of the Avonlea highway,
#334, Ursulescu's were the original owners. *(Mar. 8, 2000)*

West of the
March 8 sketch location on highway #334, this set of deteriorating buildings is located a mile south of the grid. They are the original buildings of the Dobrichan family. *(Mar. 9, 2000)*

On this day I watched five mule deer wandering across a summerfallow field west of Milestone. When they arrived in front of these old buildings I added them to the composition. *(Mar. 10, 2000)*

On a trip to Springside to visit our son and family, my sketching board, paper and pencils were standard equipment. Early in the morning I took the opportunity to drive north of Springside to sketch this old cream-coloured stucco house and wooden garage. *(Mar. 11, 2000)*

An old log house northeast of Springside, just a few patches of the whitewashed covering remain. Note the older part on the west and the newer addition on the east. *(Mar. 12, 2000)*

Just down the road from the
March 12 sketch location stands another log house with a shingled exterior. Most of the shingles are missing, but the house is still sturdy despite the passage of time. *(Mar. 13, 2000)*

It was snowing heavily as I sketched this barn north of Kronau. The whiteness of the snow gave the grey exterior a ghostlike appearance. *(Mar. 14, 2000)*

Located southwest of Wilcox, this little house and faded red barn nestle in a sea of tall grass. *(Mar. 15, 2000)*

West of the March 15 sketch, this building with its tall cindercrete chimney, and missing its red rolled roofing, was all that remained in the farmyard. *(Mar. 16, 2000)*

Located south of Milestone on the west side of highway #6, the afternoon sun casts long tree shadows on the little farmhouse. *(Mar. 17, 2000)*

This barn and sagging lean-to northeast of Parry are deteriorating through lack of repair, the elements and time. *(Mar. 18, 2000)*

Northwest of the
March 18 sketch site, this
house with its dark aged cedar siding is a strong contrast
to the bleached barn
minus all its shingles. *(Mar. 19, 2000)*

On a cool
overcast afternoon, dead hollyhock stalks
line the south side of the weathered Scherrer house northwest
of Parry. The lean-to on the shed housed chickens at one time.
(Mar. 20, 2000)

North of the
March 20 sketch location stands the
vacant Max Kesslering farmyard with its dark asphalt
composition house and polled fence. *(Mar. 21, 2000)*

Northeast of
Truax, above a little valley
buffeted by the prairie winds, stands
what remains of the Nichol farm. I remember being in this house as a
young boy. The kitchen on the sunlit side is gone. This is an example of
how quickly pioneer homes can disappear. *(Mar. 22, 2000)*

The weathered old Molleken house is located a mile and a half south of the junction of highways #6 and #39 east of Corinne. *(Mar. 23, 2000)*

I walked a half-mile from a road to sketch the Hiles home northeast of Truax, just outside of the community pasture. A beautiful bright day, with no snow, it was very warm for March. *(Mar. 24, 2000)*

This asphalt brick-patterned house south of Wilcox is dwarfed by the huge poplar tree. The telltale privy indicates there was no running water.
(Mar. 25, 2000)

The Schultz barn with its metal-clad roof and partial metal front is located south of Wilcox.
(Mar. 26, 2000)

On the Parry grid west of highway #6 stands a shop owned by Wilfred Matchett. The storage tank indicates it was once heated by oil. This building was the original Hawthorne School. *(Mar. 27, 2000)*

West of the Matchett building,
L.P. Nielsons' white barn was originally a school barn.
It was moved onto his property. *(Mar. 28. 2000)*

On the eastern outskirts of
Parry, this white-trimmed red barn with black roof
belongs to Wendell and Joan Lindstrom. *(Mar. 29, 2000)*

This splendid old
red barn with white trim is located west
of Corinne on highway 334. AK-SAR-BEN is Nebraska
spelled backwards. *(Mar. 30, 2000)*

PICKERING
MAR. 30, 2000

Located west of Parry, two old barns
and a shop are becoming more dilapidated. *(Mar. 31, 2000)*

These buildings are located west of Truax on a grid
road on the edge of a coulee. Bright sunshine creates a
contrast to the approaching rain. *(April 1, 2000)*

Heavy snow blots out much of the detail on the McCabe house west of Dummer.
(April 2, 2000)

This house in Darwin and Pat Downing's yard is his grandfather's original homestead. On the sunlit side was a lean-to, now gone. Notice the stovepipe hole in the wall. I've drawn this sketch as it would have looked in 1901 on the wide open expanse of prairie.
(April 3, 2000)

PICKERING
APRIL,3,2000

Built in 1913, this was the second house on the Downing farm south of Corinne. *(April 4, 2000)*

This Downing barn is north of the original homestead. Wilcox is visible in the distance. *(April 5, 2000)*

This faded red barn is located almost straight west of Milestone as the crow flies. Robert and Judy Moorhead live on the property. *(April 6, 2000)*

All that is left of the Tom Love farm southwest of Milestone is this old barn. Minus shingles, the roof is covered in orange lichen. The Town of Milestone is on the horizon. *(April 7, 2000)*

M. Gilchrist's white barn stands on a hill southwest of Corinne. *(April 8, 2000)*

This old collapsing house was originally made of logs, then covered with siding. It is in the Kisbey/Forget area on highway #13. *(April 9, 2000)*

This house is east of Stoughton and a half-mile south of highway #13. *(April 10, 2000)*

This collapsed barn with a fallen cupola is in the same yard as the April 10 sketch. *(April 11, 2000)*

Located on the north side of highway #13 in the Arcola/Kisbey area, this building leans away from the prevailing wind. *(April 12, 2000)*

This old bank building was moved to a farm one mile west of Bengough. The radiator in the entryway shows that the bank had steam heat. *(April 13, 2000)*

East of
Bengough and
south of the Four Corners
intersection, I came upon this little low house.
The sparse tattered pieces hanging on the exterior are
orange asphalt siding. *(April 14, 2000)*

On the east side of the grid across from the
April 14 sketch is this weather worn house with
the collapsed lean-to. Note the support for
the chimney. *(April 15, 2000)*

Traveling east of the Four Corners near Bengough, this house with its noticeable addition on the south side is another vacant farmstead. *(April 16, 2000)*

Continuing east of the Four Corners, this feedlot with its board fence windbreak stands empty of livestock. *(April 17, 2000)*

The Chris Johnson house on the Dummer grid casts shadows from an afternoon sun. *(April 18, 2000)*

West of the Village of Dummer, this house was owned by William Tulloch, a well-known water witcher. *(April 19, 2000)*

This barn
south of Wilcox had black asphalt shingles; some are missing because of the wind and weather. At one time it was part of the Rich farm. *(April 20, 2000)*

An early morning sketch north of highway #334, the town of Wilcox is in the distance. *(April 21, 2000)*

The McCrystal barn is west of Milestone near the Moose Jaw River. *(April 22, 2000)*

This red barn with white trim and adjacent chicken house are part of a heritage farm owned by the Hubbs family. *(April 23, 2000)*

PICKERING
APRIL 23, 2000

The Heims farm is on highway #334 southwest of Wilcox. Shadows from an early morning sun contrast the clean white house with its green roof. *(April 24, 2000)*

PICKERING
APRIL 24, 2000

The Fraser house belonged to our good neighbours a mile west of our farm southwest of Wilcox. Although the house is long gone, I sketched it from an earlier (1971) acrylic painting. *(April 25, 2000)*

PICKERING
APRIL 25, 2000

Northwest of Parry is the former home of Ernie Kesslering, who presently lives across the alley from our home in Milestone. *(April 26, 2000)*

East of Parry, I sketched the Broughton barn, including their saddle horse. *(April 27, 2000)*

Another
Downing farm north
of Milestone, this was once the summer home of
Leighton Downing. *(April 28, 2000)*

Southwest
of Milestone,
Clair Treleaven's
house stands vacant
in the snow.
(April 29, 2000)

The Ross Wright barn northwest of Milestone sits on the top of a rise. *(April 30, 2000)*

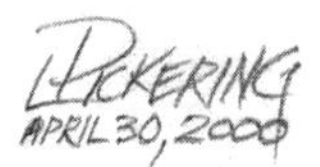

I could not resist sketching this barn north of Milestone. The "Go-pher Broke Farm" sign and overall-clad gopher indicate this farmer has a vivid sense of humour. *(May 1, 2000)*

Another 100-year-old heritage barn in George and Pat Smith's farmyard northeast of Milestone. *(May 2, 2000)*

The Pat and Margaret Baker house, shed and barn are north of Milestone. *(May 3, 2000)*

This vacant grey asphalt-brick covered house is along highway #334 east of Avonlea. *(May 4, 2000)*

A cloudy sky and signs of rain are the setting for this white hip-roofed barn with green trim northeast of Milestone. The roof on the near side is breaking away from the front. *(May 5, 2000)*

Northwest
of the May 5 sketch
location, the house and shed are all that remain of the
Sherman farm. *(May 6, 2000)*

Northeast of Milestone, the original barn has had the
walls lowered and is used now as a machine shed.
Note the old cook car on the west side; it was
used during the days of
threshing machines.
(May 7, 2000)

This neat white barn in the Ballman yard northeast of Milestone is still being used for horses. Note the Collie dog lying in the shade.
(May 8, 2000)

The Frank and Leah Kime buildings sit atop a rise northeast of Milestone. The south-facing verandah casts a deep shadow in the morning light.
(May 9, 2000)

Also on a slight rise northeast of Milestone are Leland Metz's former house and barn. *(May 10, 2000)*

Located southwest of Parry, the barn is all that is left in the Crawford farmyard. *(May 11, 2000)*

The Monte Kesslering farmstead is nestled against the Parry Hills. The buildings on the right seem to be defying gravity, and will soon collapse from the elements. *(May 12, 2000)*

Driving east on a grid road south of Parry, I sketched the Andrew Wingert barn. *(May 13, 2000)*

This house stands on a knoll southwest of Parry. *(May 14, 2000)*

The Fullmores, who operated a store in Parry, built these two houses on the grid west of the town. *(May 15, 2000)*

Located north of Avonlea on a grid
road, this barn has a cement bottom and wooden
top. The barn seems to have double or triple landings. *(May 16, 2000)*

Standing in a field northwest of Avonlea, this
building was used for grain storage.
With the dormer on the east, could
it have been a dwelling at one
time? (*May 17, 2000)*

Driving west and north of the May 17 sketch location, I came upon this three-story house with huge dead poplars in the foreground. Locals informed me that Ray Patterson was the owner.
(May 18, 2000)

Northeast of Avonlea I added this rather worn red barn to my sketch collection.
(May 19, 2000)

Enroute to Edmonton,
this barnyard was sketched near Marsden on highway #40. *(May 20, 2000)*

This old sway-backed barn east of Marsden had shifted partially off its fieldstone and cement foundation.
(May 21 , 2000)

A cloudy sky with a stiff breeze from the northwest was the setting of this barn along highway #40. *(May 22, 2000)*

As we drove east on highway #40, we came across this country school. The name "Smilesville" says it all. *(May 23, 2000)*

A strong southeast wind blew as I sketched the Blaine Renwick barn east of Corinne. *(May 24, 2000)*

The Ken and Florence Renwick barn is also east of Corinne. *(May 25, 2000)*

Darryl Jacobs' large barn stands on a slight rise north of Milestone. *(May 26, 2000)*

The W.W. Pedersen barn is north of the May 26 sketch location. The walls have been lowered for use as a machine shed. (M*ay 27, 2000)*

Continuing north, the amount
of orange lichen on the roofs of
this set of buildings indicate their age.
(May 28, 2000)

A country church in the town of Kayville.
(May 29, 2000)

The Ballou barn stands on highway #6 north of Corinne. *(May 30, 2000)*

This large house west of Riceton is minus its roof. *(May 31, 2000)*

A large barn south of Estlin. *(June 1, 2000)*

Old and new – a steel grain bin and a barn north of Milestone. *(June 2, 2000)*

This house stands west of Riceton on the main grid. *(June 3, 2000)*

It was a bright sunny morning when I made this sketch. Two weeks later the elevator was torn down. How fast the landscape changes! *(June 4, 2000)*

This barn is on the north side of the grid road west of Riceton. *(June 5, 2000)*

A very different design for another barn on the grid road west of Riceton. *(June 6, 2000)*

This barn is east of the borders of the municipalities of Lajord #128 and Scott #98. *(June 7, 2000)*

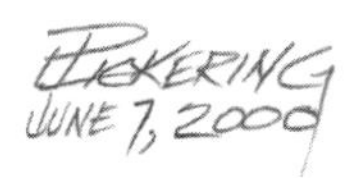

South of Riceton on the grid, this barn is situated on a slight rise. *(June 8, 2000)*

Note the lean on this abandoned farmhouse in the Estlin area. *(June 9, 2000)*

South of Riceton, this white barn with green roof was lowered for machinery storage. The old house has collapsed. *(June 10, 2000)*

These two fine cream-coloured barns on the outskirts of Lang are owned by Bob and Mabel Howlett. *(June 11, 2000)*

After heavy rains, I had to stick to blacktop driving. This barn is on the north side of highway #39, east of Lang. *(June 12, 2000)*

This red barn with a green roof
is east of Lang. *(June 13, 2000)*

On the west side of
Lang, this barn is within the town limits.
(June 14, 2000)

On the east side
of Lang, this barn is also within the town limits.
(June 15, 2000)

PICKERING
JUNE 15, 2000

North of the correction line on the
east side of highway #6 to
Regina, this large barn has a
distinctive weather vane.
(June 16, 2000)

PICKERING
JUNE 16, 2000

On highway #6 south, this house is noted for being used for posting numerous election campaign and graduation signs. *(June 17, 2000)*

North of the junction of highways #6 and #13 stands this white house with blue gable ends. *(June 18, 2000)*

The Pool elevator at Pangman, this classic prairie scene is disappearing.
(June 19, 2000)

South of the #6 and #13 highway junction is this grain storage building. I presume it was a barn at one time.
(June 20, 2000)

South of Milestone on highway #6, it was raining heavily with a stiff breeze. I had my car window down, thus the blotchy raindrops on my drawing. *(June 21, 2000)*

North of Ceylon
and west of highway #6 on
a grid road, the afternoon sun created a
long dark shadow on the front of the barn.
(June 22, 2000)

The home of George Anderson, former Federal Elevator agent, stands on the outskirts of Milestone. *(June 23, 2000)*

The Hugh Kenyon farmyard is on highway #6 southwest of Milestone.
(June 24, 2000)

On highway #13, east of the junction of #6, this house stands in a field on the north side of the highway. *(June 25, 2000)*

I drove south down a very muddy road west of Khedive to sketch this old barn.
(June 26, 2000)

This old barn on the Garnet Moore ranch is located east and south of the Khedive turnoff. *(June 27, 2000)*

This weather beaten barn is nestled in a little valley east and north of Ogema. *(June 28, 2000)*

South of the June 28th
sketch location, also in the valley, this bleached barn stands near a little marsh. *(June 29, 2000)*

East of Ogema, just north of the tracks, this white house with green trim stands on a rise on the west side of the road. While making this sketch, a R.C.M.P. officer pulled up and inquired, "Are you Gordon?" Before I could answer, he added, "Oh, you're sketching." Wishing me a good day, he continued on his way, the local officer just doing his duty in a Crime Watch area. *(June 30, 2000)*

A mile north of the June 30 sketch
location, sharp dark afternoon shadows gave a feeling of depth
beneath the verandah roof. *(July 1, 2000)*

This cedar-sided house, with extensive additions,
is located north of Indian Head on
highway # 56. *(July 2, 2000)*

Near a marsh north of Indian Head, this barn is the only building on the property. *(July 3, 2000)*

The Bell Farm historic round barn is located on highway #56 north of Indian Head. *(July 4, 2000)*

This barn and attached shed are east of Kronau. *(July 5, 2000)*

The Button farmhouse is on highway #334 south of Wilcox. *(July 6, 2000)*

Driving to Melfort, I sketched this barn with its round conical cupola along highway #6 north of Southey. *(July 7, 2000)*

This house stands on a hill above the barn in the July 7 sketch. *(July 8, 2000)*

This log house, with part of its plastered walls missing, is located along highway #6 south of Melfort. *(July 9, 2000)*

The J. Baker barn is on the west side of highway #6 south of Regina. *(July 10, 2000)*

The Pioneer elevator at Estlin has had several additions. *(July 11, 2000)*

The Allen Sambrook barn is south of Milestone. *(July 12, 2000)*

The Carl Weisshaar Sr. former family home is south of Regina, one mile east and one mile south of the correction line on highway #6.
(July 13, 2000)

This barn and old granaries are in the Rowatt/Estlin area. *(July 14, 2000)*

Old square wooden grain bins are becoming a thing of the past, these four wooden structures are located east of Milestone. *(July 15, 2000)*

The Gary Bradley house is southeast of Milestone. *(July 16, 2000)*

This early Pool elevator was demolished in February 2001. At one time Milestone had eight elevators. Only one remains. These town landmarks will soon disappear, leaving only highway signs to identify the towns and villages. *(July 17, 2000)*

Two old grain bins southeast of Milestone are surrounded by the ever-present dock. *(July 18, 2000)*

PICKERING
JULY 18, 2000

These two grain bins were built by my Grandfather. No longer in use, they still stand on his original homestead south of Wilcox. *(July 19, 2000)*

Afternoon shadows stand in sharp relief on this barn northeast of Estlin. *(July 20, 2000)*

This house and barn are east of Rowatt on the south side of a grid road. *(July 21, 2000)*

Streaked and faded, this red barn is northeast of Rowatt. *(July 22, 2000)*

This farmyard is northeast of Lang. *(July 23, 2000)*

Well weathered, this white cottage-roofed house is west of Lewvan. *(July 24, 2000)*

A partial metal roof survives on this
old leaning red barn east of Rowatt. *(July 25, 2000)*

This old
grain bin southwest
of Milestone is no longer fit for storage. *(July 26, 2000)*

This imitation-brick-clad house is northeast of Lang. *(July 27, 2000)*

This tall cottage-roofed house is southeast of Estlin. *(July 28, 2000)*

This Estlin-area barn has a metal-clad roof.
(July 29, 2000)

PICKERING
JULY 29, 2000

The dead tree to the left of this little cedar-shingled house in the Lewvan area echoes its desolation.
(July 30, 2000)

PICKERING
JULY 30, 2000

White trim outlines this red barn in the Estlin area. *(July 31, 2000)*

This white barn is east of the highway #6 correction line south of Regina. *(Aug. 1, 2000)*

A historic reminder of early times, this horse-drawn wagon stands above the banks of the Moose Jaw River on the Rennick farm south of Milestone. *(Aug. 2, 2000)*

Lowered for use as a machine shed, this barn is located east of the highway #6 correction line. *(Aug. 3, 2000)*

This farmyard with a tall windmill, once used to pump water, is in the Estlin area. *(Aug. 4, 2000)*

The kitchen is all that remains of the Howell farmhouse east of Dummer. *(Aug. 5, 2000)*

I used an old photo to create this sketch of my Grandfather Robert Lewis's house at Raymore. *(Aug. 6, 2000)*

Another barn in the Estlin area lowered for farm equipment storage. *(Aug. 7, 2000)*

This barn and outbuildings are east of Rowatt. *(Aug. 8, 2000)*

This weathered low white house with green asphalt shingles is located in the Estlin area. *(Aug. 9, 2000)*

In the Estlin area, this house and barn look long abandoned. (*Aug. 10, 2000*)

This house east of Rowatt has been converted to an equipment shed. (*Aug. 11, 2000*)

This Parrish and Heimbecker elevator is at Lewvan.
(Aug. 12, 2000)

The Kendal/Odessa area is the location of this old farmhouse.
(Aug. 13, 2000)

Just the bare framework remains of the lean-to attached to this barn in the Lewvan area. *(Aug. 14, 2000)*

Towering above this weathered white barn in the Lewvan area, the old windmill at one time pumped water from a well. All the blades are missing from the huge fan. Note the silhouette of a horse attached to the fan. *(Aug. 15, 2000)*

This farmhouse stands in the same yard as the barn in the August 15 sketch. *(Aug. 16, 2000)*

A farmyard northeast of Lang. *(Aug. 17, 2000)*

In contrast to some prairie farmsteads, this farmstead northeast of Lewvan is well treed. *(Aug. 18, 2000)*

Returning from Calgary, I sketched this little house perched above the south ditch on highway #1 near Cluny, Alberta. (*Aug. 19, 2000*)

This collapsed old barn tucked behind rows of hay bales is in Alberta just off highway #1.
(Aug. 20, 2000)

This old house and log barn are on the east side of highway #41 near Elkwater Park, Alberta.
(Aug. 21, 2000)

With my camera,
I walked into a
pasture on the west side of
highway #41 in Alberta to photograph this old log house as a reference for this sketch. *(Aug. 22, 2000)*

On top of a hill near highway #41, I photographed this cream-coloured school house and sway-backed barn. It brought back memories, as I had attended a country school as a boy. (*Aug. 23, 2000)*

Back in Saskatchewan, Cypress Hills West Block, I found this old log ranch dwelling on the banks of the Battle River. *(Aug. 24, 2000)*

On the edge of Reed Lake, between Herbert and Morse, is this abandoned shed. *(Aug. 25, 2000)*

North of highway #1, east of Gull Lake, I sketched this ranch. The house is on the top of a ravine and the barn is tucked in at the bottom.
(Aug. 26, 2000)

In the same area as the August 26 sketch is this dilapidated chicken house. *(Aug. 27, 2000)*

This large barn is in the same yard as the August 27 sketch.
(Aug. 28, 2000)

This house stands high on a cutbank on the north side of highway #1 at Parkbeg.
(Aug. 29, 2000)

Peter Nepper once owned this barn west of Wilcox.
(Aug. 30, 2000)

Here is the Nepper house as it exists today.
(Aug. 31, 2000)

Wilbur Drew's house is south of Wilcox. *(Sept. 1, 2000)*

This old school stands above the valley south of Fort Qu'Appelle. *(Sept. 2, 2000)*

Many of the exterior cedar shingles are missing on the sunlit side of this house near Truax. The chimney is gone from the orange-coloured lichen-strewn roof. *(Sept. 3, 2000)*

Truax still has its Pool elevator. *(Sept. 4, 2000)*

This hip-roofed faded red barn with its nine-paned windows is located in the Parry/Dummer area.
(Sept. 5, 2000)

Surrounded by durum wheat, this house in the Dummer/Parry area is minus its two chimneys. *(Sept. 6, 2000)*

These pioneers located their farmyard on top of a hill in rolling terrain in the Hardy area. *(Sept. 7, 2000)*

Again in the Hardy area, this lean-to has collapsed. *(Sept. 8, 2000)*

The evening sunlight created shadows on the dormers of this white stucco house near the Ceylon campground where we camped for the night in our van. *(Sept. 9, 2000)*

I drove to the junction of highways #6 and #13 to tank up with gas. On to Parry to photograph the Parry elevator for this sketch. *(Sept. 10, 2000)*

Heading south to Ceylon, we turned west of highway #6 and photographed this asphalt brick schoolhouse which is now surrounded by a grain field. *(Sept. 11, 2000)*

This barn south of Ceylon on highway #6 is surrounded by a summerfallowed field. *(Sept. 12, 2000)*

On the west side of highway #6 I walked in and photographed this wide, faded red barn perched atop a hill. *(Sept. 13, 2000)*

Located on the west side of highway #6 north of Minton, this cottage-roofed house perched on a hill is clad in cedar shingles. *(Sept. 14, 2000)*

This dark cedar-sided building is in the Minton area.
(Sept. 15, 2000)

This barn with its multiple additions is located in the Minton area. *(Sept. 16, 2000)*

East of Minton, on highway #18 toward Gladmar, this collapsed building sits in a valley. The poled corral suggests it could have been a line shack. *(Sept. 17, 2000)*

After touring the Town of Lake Alma, we headed north and east toward Colgate, and I added this red barn to the collection. *(Sept. 18, 2000)*

Enroute
to Colgate,
we came across
this house on the
north side of the
road. The roof was a vivid orange in the late
afternoon sunshine and a red fox emerged from
the adjacent wheat field. *(Sept. 19, 2000)*

After touring
Colgate and its famous golf course,
I turned north on highway #35, adding this metal-clad-
roofed, cement-bottomed barn to my collection.
(Sept.20 , 2000)

This partial fieldstone cemented red barn is located south of Weyburn. *(Sept. 21, 2000)*

Northwest of Avonlea, built on a hill, this multi-windowed dark, cedar-sided house presented a strong contrast to the fall sky. *(Sept. 22, 2000)*

The dramatic
slope of the roof of this long barn northwest of
Avonlea shows the inevitable decline of age.
(Sept. 23, 2000)

This house is in the same yard as the September 23 sketch.
The fuel storage tank indicates it was heated by oil.
(Sept. 24, 2000)

In the mid-thirties, my Grandfather moved from the farm south of Wilcox to a farm south of Katepwa Lake. All that remains of this barn is the cement bottom. *(Sept. 25, 2000)*

My Grandfather's weather beaten house is in the same yard as the remains of the barn. *(Sept. 26, 2000)*

This three-storied house south of Indian Head is the Gun Club. *(Sept. 27, 2000)*

The top of the cupola is missing on this red barn located in the Kendal area. *(Sept. 28, 2000)*

This barn is located in the Francis area.
(Sept. 29, 2000)

This house is in the same yard as the September 29 sketch. *(Sept. 30, 2000)*

This lowered barn in the Francis area was used for grain storage, thus the cross-section braces. *(Oct. 1, 2000)*

This cottage-roofed house in the Kendal/Francis area at one time had a 32-volt windcharger for electricity. *(Oct. 2, 2000)*

The orange lichen on the roof of this Kendal/Francis area house shows its age.
(Oct. 3, 2000)

This tall brick-covered house, with its steep roofed dormer, is located in the Francis area.
(Oct. 4, 2000)

This cream-coloured stucco house in the Francis area has a red roof. *(Oct. 5, 2000)*

Early snow cloaks this red barn built into a bank northwest of Avonlea. *(Oct. 6, 2000)*

At
this house
northwest of Avonlea, and west of the Blue Hills church,
my wife and I met Larry Jeffrey who gave us some
information about the area. *(Oct. 7, 2000)*

Traveling west, I walked south into a little valley to reach
this house. An old truck was abandoned on the east side.
(Oct. 8, 2000)

This leaning barn is in the same yard as the house shown in the October 8 sketch. *(Oct. 9, 2000)*

We continued on west to the Jim Jeffrey ranch. In my sketch I did a little restoration on the ranch exterior, covering it with siding. *(Oct. 10, 2000)*

The Hipper Holme School was moved from further west. It now rests on the Jeffrey property.
(Oct. 11, 2000)

Leaving the Jeffrey Ranch we headed east, stopping to add this house with its low lean-tos. We then drove to Crane Valley and camped for the night.
(Oct. 12, 2000)

A long morning chimney shadow is cast across the roof of this garage and shop near Crane Valley. *(Oct. 13, 2000)*

The red brick chimney top has fallen into a crumbled heap on the roof of this house in the Crane Valley area. *(Oct. 14, 2000)*

This barn is part of the farmyard in the October 14 sketch. *(Oct. 15, 2000)*

Turning south off a grid road in the Crane Valley area, we came across this house with many of the cedar shingles missing from the east side. *(Oct. 16, 2000)*

This shed is in the same yard, northeast of the house sketched on October 16. *(Oct. 17, 2000)*

On top of a hill, south of the two previous sketches, was this cedar-shingled building used for grain storage. It appeared to have been a barn at one time. *(Oct. 18, 2000)*

We drove back to a grid going east toward highway #36, and stopped to add this sketch of a garage on the north side of the road. *(Oct. 19, 2000)*

This barn is part of the same Crane Valley area yard as the October 16 sketch. *(Oct. 20, 2000)*

An old wagon sits
beside this house with asphalt imitation brick siding in
the Crane Valley/Cardross area. *(Oct. 21, 2000)*

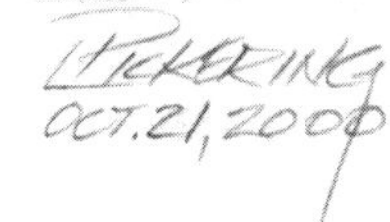

This building in the Cardross area was probably
a barn. At one time it may have been used for
grain storage. *(Oct. 22, 2000)*

I walked into a field to add this double dormer building set into a bank in the Cardross area. It was possibly used for grain storage. *(Oct. 23, 2000)*

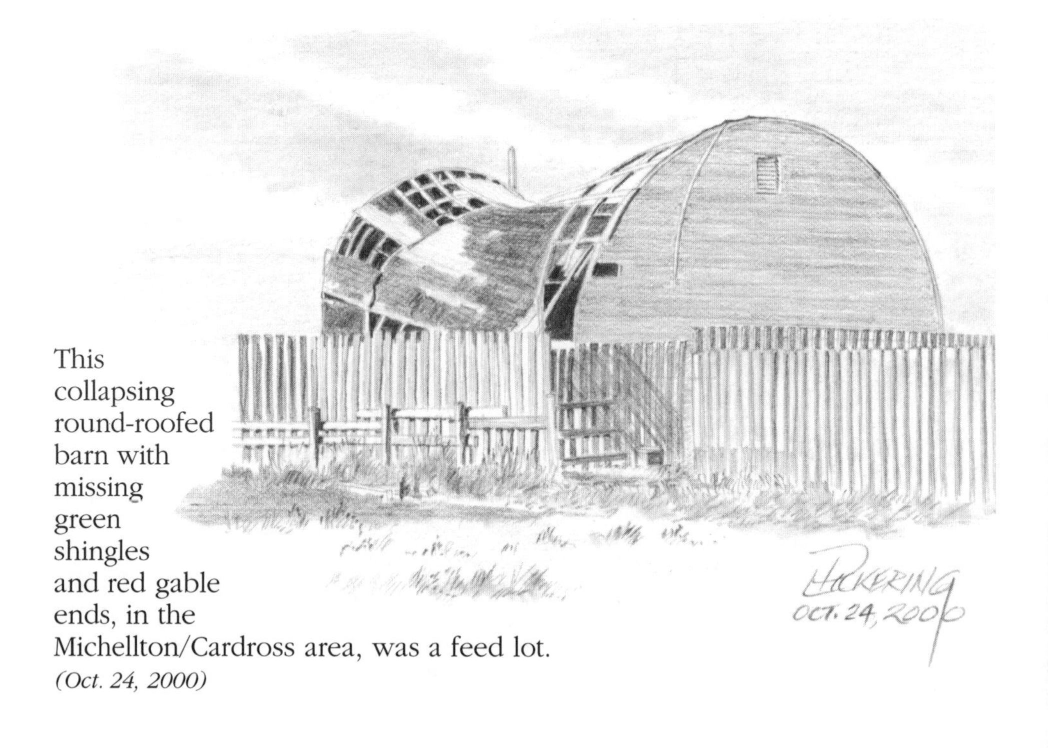

This collapsing round-roofed barn with missing green shingles and red gable ends, in the Michellton/Cardross area, was a feed lot. *(Oct. 24, 2000)*

This old grey barn is in the Mitchellton area.
(Oct. 25, 2000)

This cottage-roofed house is also near Michellton. *(Oct. 26, 2000)*

This old bunkhouse, in an abandoned ranch yard northwest of Crane Valley, has a swaybacked roof and shingles missing from its cedar exterior. As I photographed this building I thought of the early cowboys who bunked within, with its wood-burning stove and drafty walls. As I headed toward the old barn, I imagined the sound of a mouth organ breaking the stillness. *(Oct. 27. 2000)*

This old barn, in the same yard as the October 27 sketch, was built on a cement foundation facing east toward a hillside. The eastern doorway was chewed by porcupines. All that remained of the ranch house was a basement. The house may have been moved away. *(Oct. 28, 2000)*

Driving east to highway #36, I noticed this lone little house high on the valley wall. Looking through the east window I saw a coffee pot and a Chase and Sanborn coffee can on the stove. *(Oct. 29, 2000)*

North of Crane Valley, on the east bank of highway #36, is this old store with a garage and living quarters. *(Oct. 30, 2000)*

Opposite the store in the October 30 sketch, this old cottage-roofed house stands on a high bank against a cloudy sky. *(Oct. 31, 2000)*

West of Bayard, an evening sky is the setting for this faded white house with a blue banded bottom. (N*ov. 1, 2000)*

This long low house is northwest of Avonlea. *(Nov. 2, 2000)*

Another long house
northwest of Avonlea.
Note the many windows. *(Nov. 3, 2000)*

This cottage-roofed house south of Milestone was the home of William Rennick. (*Nov. 4, 2000)*

A snow storm creates a ghost-like appearance in this lowered red barn which is in the same yard as the house in the November 4 sketch.
(Nov. 5, 2000)

The Maitland Ross barn west of Milestone has a fitting name as it was built in the Caledonia municipality. *(Nov. 6, 2000)*

Located southwest of Wilcox, this was the home of Andrew Kvisle. *(Nov. 7, 2000)*

This barn in the Kayville area leans away from the prevailing wind. *(Nov. 8, 2000)*

Set on a hill in the Kayville area this barn was missing many shingles. *(Nov. 9, 2000)*

This old barn rests on top of a hill northwest of Avonlea with the Blue Hills in the background. *(Nov. 10, 2000)*

This garage and shop are in the same yard as the November 10 sketch. *(Nov. 11, 2000)*

This collapsed shed is located on highway
#368, on the outskirts of the little village of Pathlow. *(Nov. 12, 2000)*

Returning from a family visit to Melfort, I found this faded red barn, with its snow-covered roof, near Pathlow. *(Nov. 13, 2000)*

Located on the west side of highway #368, south of St. Brieux, this log barn shows very little deterioration. *(Nov. 14, 2000)*

This log chicken house is in the same yard as the November 14 sketch. *(Nov. 15, 2000)*

These two grain bins are northeast of Lake Lenore. *(Nov. 16, 2000)*

Deep shadows add drama to the empty cavernous hayloft of this barn west of Watson. *(Nov. 17, 2000)*

This large house is on the west side of highway #6 south of Raymore. *(Nov. 18, 2000)*

This small house is situated near Claybank. *(Nov. 19, 2000)*

Howard and Edie Ross own this red barn west of Milestone. The barn is built into the banks of the Moose Jaw River valley. On the north end a ramp leads into the hayloft. *(Nov. 20, 2000)*

Eldon Terry's barn is southwest of Milestone. *(Nov. 21, 2000)*

Across
from Eldon
and Lorraine Terry's farmyard stands
Jake Strand's original homestead, including the wrought-iron
bedstead. *(Nov. 22, 2000)*

This barn west of Corinne and north on
the Rouleau grid was sketched on a
bright, mild day. *(Nov. 23, 2000)*

This barn north on the Rouleau grid has the remains of a what may have been a chicken house on the east side. *(Nov. 24, 2000)*

On the same location as the November 24 sketch stands this little cottage-roofed house. *(Nov. 25, 2000)*

From highway #34, south of Avonlea, I walked down a winding lane to this ochre Insulbrick dwelling. The tall north section was built first. The later addition still has its exterior shingles. *(Nov. 26, 2000)*

I walked a mile from highway #334 to this grey Insulbrick house on top of a hill. While walking around the building, I stepped into a badger hole right up to my knees, and fell backwards. Shaken, I headed back to my van thinking about what I would have done with a broken leg! *(Nov. 27, 2000)*

Heavy snow fell on this grey barn in the Kayville area. *(Nov. 28, 2000)*

On the top of a hill southeast of Kayville, this old house is minus all of its windows and doors.
(Nov. 29, 2000)

This building is east of Claybank. Defying the elements, it now serves as a shelter for the cow looking out of the opening. *(Nov. 30, 2000)*

I located this house in a rolling terrain pasture on the grid east of Kayville. The hinges on the frame of the west side upper window, and the braced platform, seem to indicate a fire escape. *(Dec. 1, 2000)*

A dropping sun casts tree shadows on this collapsed barn northwest of Kayville. *(Dec. 2, 2000)*

Across the road from the December 2 sketch this partially clad metal-covered building shone in the crisp afternoon air. *(Dec. 3, 2000)*

In the same area, strong shadows look dramatic against the sunlit front of this building. *(Dec. 4, 2000)*

Harsh winter shadows fall on the end of this doomed building in the same area as the three previous sketches *(Dec. 5, 2000)*

This house near Kayville has a fieldstone and cement foundation. The exterior was covered in grey asphalt siding.
(Dec. 6, 2000)

East of Kayville, this rusty red building with white-trimmed windows was used for grain storage. It appeared to have been be a railroad building at one time. *(Dec. 7, 2000)*

This white stucco
house sat in a farmyard near Kayville.
(Dec. 8, 2000)

Near Kayville, long late-afternoon shadows left the west side of this barn very dark. A winter moon hangs in the eastern sky. *(Dec. 9, 2000)*

The Drew barn is south of Wilcox. *(Dec. 10, 2000)*

This cream-coloured hip-roofed barn is in the Drinkwater area. *(Dec. 11, 2000)*

This brick-patterned asphalt exterior cottage-roofed house is northwest of Drinkwater. *(Dec. 12, 2000)*

Double lean-tos add an almost elegant look to this red barn located in the same yard as the house in the December 12 sketch. *(Dec. 13, 2000)*

This odd-shaped building sits in a field east of Tuxford. It may have been used for grain storage.
(Dec. 14, 2000)

With a missing metal cupola, this barn sits in a little hollow west of highway #2 north of Tuxford. *(Dec. 15, 2000)*

The lower part of this barn was constructed of cement, the upper loft area of wood. It is southwest of Tuxford. *(Dec. 16, 2000)*

This dilapidated shingle-clad barn is on the edge of a ravine east of highway #2, south of Chamberlain. *(Dec. 17, 2000)*

These two buildings are just west of the
December 17 barn sketch.
(Dec. 18, 2000)

On the west side of highway #2, north of
Tuxford, this building is used for grain storage.
Chimney holes seem to indicate that it was once a
house. *(Dec. 19, 2000)*

I walked down the lane toward a farmyard in the Marquis/Tuxford area to see this beautiful house built of fieldstones. The various colours of the stones – reds, browns, blacks, greens, greys and creams – made a dramatic contrast to the usual wooden prairie farmhouses. (*Dec. 20, 2000)*

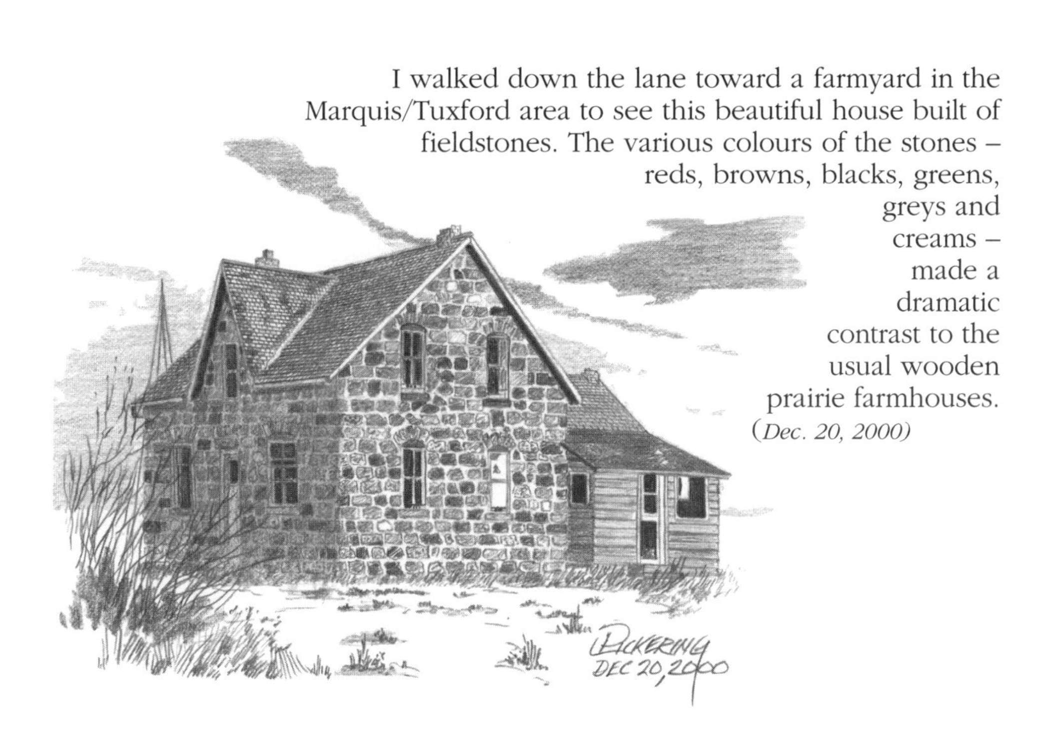

Just north of the stone house in the December 20 sketch, this red barn has one cupola leaning and the other resting on the metal-clad roof, giving it a whimsical look. *(Dec. 21, 2000)*

Halfway up the wall of the Qu'Appelle Valley, on the north side of Buffalo Pound Lake, sits this faded red double lean-to hip-roofed barn. *(Dec. 22, 2000)*

This large three-story faded white house is located northwest of Tuxford on highway #42. The verandah is missing from the east side. *(Dec. 23, 2000)*

Located
southwest of
the Tuxford/Marquis area,
this barn has cupolas with an unusual shape.
Galvanized metal covers the roof.
(Dec. 24, 2000)

The old hayrake backed into the front door adds an unusual note to this faded white house with green trim in the Tuxford/Marquis area.
(Dec. 25, 2000)

This oil-heated home is in the same yard as the Chamberlain-area sketches dated December 17 and 18. *(Dec. 26, 2000)*

This white farmhouse is northwest of Rouleau. *(Dec. 27, 2000)*

The G.L. Patterson farmhouse was west of Dummer. *(Dec. 28, 2000)*

My wife's grandparents, Frank and Elsie Howell, lived in this farmhouse which was situated above the bank of the Avonlea Creek east of Dummer. Mrs. Elsie Howell was the secretary-treasurer of the RM of Caledonia for 44 years. *(Dec. 29, 2000)*

East of Bengough, this low rambling house is succumbing to time and harsh prairie weather. *(Dec. 30, 2000)*

This collapsed house lies down a slope from the house in the December 30 sketch. *(Dec. 31, 2000)*

HELPFUL GIFT IDEAS

Children's Medical Emergency Handbook ________ x $18.95 = $______

Cornerstones 1 ________ x $15.95 = $ _____

Cornerstones 2 ________ x $15.95 = $ _____

Getting It Together ________ x $12.95 = $ _____

Home Tips – How to Organize Your Personal Life __ x $14.95 = $ _____

Household Hints – Environment & Energy Hints ____ x $9.95 = $ _____

Household Hints – Money & Time-Saving Hints ____ x $12.95 = $ _____

Prairie Pilgrimage – 366 Prairie Sketches ________ x $15.95 = $ _____

Work Tips – Organize Your Professional Life ______ x $14.95 = $ _____

Shipping and handling charge (total order) ________ = $ 4.00

Subtotal ________ = $ ______

In Canada add 7% GST OR 15% HST where applicable ________ = $ ______

Total enclosed ________ = $ ______

U.S. and international orders payable in U.S. funds/
Prices subject to change.

NAME: ____________________

STREET: ____________________

CITY: ____________________ PROV./STATE ____________

COUNTRY ____________________ POSTAL CODE/ZIP _______

Please make cheque or money order payable to:

THE LEADER-POST CARRIER FOUNDATION INC.
P.O. Box 2020,
1964 Park Street
Regina, Saskatchewan, Canada S4P 3G4

For fundraising or volume purchase prices, contact
THE LEADER-POST CARRIER FOUNDATION INC. at (306) 565-8344.

CHILDREN'S MEDICAL EMERGENCY HANDBOOK
by Hospitals of Regina Foundation
Professional help is at your fingertips. In a medical emergency seconds can make a difference. With this handbook you can begin emergency treatment immediately. It may help you save a life! Hospital emergency room specialists provide practical, easy-to-follow instructions with detailed illustrations.
Retail $18.95 **7" x 10"** **lay-flat coil binding**
244 pages **over 400 illustrations**

CORNERSTONES 1 – An Artist's History of the City of Regina
by William Argan with Pam Cowan
Historic commercial buildings, schools, churches, hotels, theatres, sports facilities and more. William Argan's striking illustrations bring the history of Regina alive. A pleasure to read, here is a fascinating look at the business, social, political and cultural cornerstones of Regina.
Retail $15.95 **6" x 9"** **perfect bound**
144 pages **over 150 illustrations**

CORNERSTONES 2 – An Artist's History of the City of Regina
by William Argan with Pam Cowan
Cornerstones 2 has illustrations and anecdotes for all of the City of Regina mayors, plus historic churches, hospitals, residences, schools and commercial buildings. New to this book are the illustrations and written histories of the many cultural and sporting clubs that are vital to the lives of the people of Regina. A visual feast and a pleasure to read,
Retail $15.95 **6" x 9"** **perfect bound**
144 pages **over 150 illustrations**

GETTING IT TOGETHER – How To Organize Your Work, Your Home and Yourself
by Patricia Katz
Practical ideas for managing complex lives are presented in readable chunks with a dash of humour. These organizational tips will combat stress and bring order to your home and workplace. Patricia Katz believes good organization frees your time and energy for the things and people that matter most in your life.
Retail $12.95 **6" x 9"** **perfect bound**
128 pages **100 line drawings**

HOUSEHOLD HINTS – Environmental, Energy, Money and Time-Saving Hints for Home and Garden

This Green Version of *Household Hints* provides hundreds of recycling ideas and environmentally friendly alternatives for home and garden, cleaning and maintenance problems. Many of these environmental and energy-conscious hints use low-cost, old-fashioned, common-sense remedies for everyday problems. Your budget and environment will love it.
Retail $9.95 **6" x 9"** **lay-flat coil binding**
96 pages **40 line drawings**

HOUSEHOLD HINTS – Money and Time-Saving Ideas for Home and Garden – Revised and Enlarged Edition – 10% more hints

From cleaning your chandelier crystals quickly and safely in your dishwasher, to prolonging the life of your pantihose by freezing them, through numerous cleaning, cooking, gardening, pet, beauty and health tips, *Household Hints* provides useable, useful and sometimes startling solutions to everyday problems.
Retail $12.95 **6" x 9"** **perfect bound**
144 pages **50 line drawings**

HOME TIPS – How To Organize Your Home and Personal Life
by Patricia Katz

Family and household organizational tips are the focus here. Patricia Katz has created a helpful, humourous and practical guide to help you balance housekeeping, family and personal obligations. With her good sense and great sense of humour, Patricia shows us how to take care of the essentials, get more out of life and expand our personal choices.
Retail $14.95 **6" x 9"** **perfect bound**
128 pages **fully illustrated**

WORK TIPS – How To Organize Your Professional and Business Life
by Patricia Katz

A professional speaker, trainer, consultant and columnist, Patricia Katz helps individuals and organizations to be more productive and effective. Practical suggestions are dispensed with a great sense of humour. *Work Tips* helps with professional and business organization time and stress management. Expand your personal choices, learn how to control paperwork and manage on the run with maximum efficiency.
Retail $14.95 **6" x 9"** **perfect bound**
128 pages **fully illustrated**